Flowering Skullcap

David Wheatley

for [illegible]

best wishes

[illegible]

27/2/'13

wurm press
wurmimapfel.net/wurmpress

ISBN: 978-0-9563732-2-9

Wurm Press
wurmimapfel.net/wurmpress

for Conor O'Callaghan

quickest way to Holyhead is via ta-ra

Acknowledgements

Poetry Ireland Review, *An Unofficial Roy Fisher* (ed. Peter Robinson, Shearsman Books), *London Review of Books*, *Times Literary Supplement*, *Icarus*, *The Burning Bush 2*, *College Green*, *Poetry Review*, *Cork Literary Review*, *The Yellow Nib*, *Shine On: Irish Writers for Shine* (Dedalus Press), *Architexts*, *Drift*, *Hide*, *Postcards from Hull* (all Hull City Council).

Thanks to Máirín Ní Dhonnchadha for editorial suggestions.

Cover design: Andrej Kapor

Contents

Brueghel's Proverbs

Before roasting a fart first you must catch it.
The deaf man applauds the hurdy-gurdy too.
If the sheep-fancier spurns your sheep
his heart is elsewhere. Where there is heart
there is pancreas. No one hates an idiot
like the village's second stupidest man.
It is quicker to beat your husband than walk
to the next town and write him a letter. Envy
the bathing sow on the day it rains dung.
The bishop shuts his mouth and sits on it.
The gangrenous leg knows good hacksaw work
when it feels it. The rat-trap feels it ought
to apologise for the baker's mouldy cheese.
When your pigs fly they're not coming back.
Two can shit through the same hole as cheaply as one.
The wooden spoon does not match the shape
of your backside for nothing. The condemned man's
vomit has a lucky escape. The hangman combs
his hair before putting his hood on. The gravedigger
will not be taking out ads. The old buffoon
has always got some proverb or other to hand.

Drypool in Old Photographs

1
The man on the corner repeats
at intervals down the street,
as though in a trick photographer's

loop: hands on hips, in fob
pockets, ignoring the see-through dog
ghosting along the pub wall

behind him feeding on air,
on the ghost of a promise
of gristle and bone.

2
Dawn in the brewery yard
finds ice on the dung,
the drayhorse's breath

steaming into the lens.
The barrels tumble chiming
into riverside cellars

and are sprung in a week;
the drayman's further-off
judgement day promises

the bump and jolt of a cemetery
clearance and only then
the vile dust settled at last.

3

The dog and I fall into step.
Peer through his vitreous ribs
and watch the brickwork rewind,

decade on decade. Does he
want feeding? There aren't
shadows enough to sate him.

Sharp against my ribs too,
the ghost of a torn-down future
pushes, prods, and will out.

A Pint of Milk

leaving behind   only yourself   and the door
unlocked
venture down   the avenue
for the messages   becoming the street
as you go   and keeping an eye out for

a hole in your shoe   the dog's   first word
a bundle of rye   tomorrow's paper
a pub with no beer   a hole in the sky

they're not just coming the convoy of
mobility buggies
they're coming
for you

the cash machine keypad scalds to the touch in the heat
the printed balance slips you   a ransom note for your money

then visit in no particular order

hair nail tanning salons   bookie's grocer's off-licence
and video shop as the mood takes you
in search of

a bottle of stubble   tomato polish
a half-pound of sun   God's own apostrophe
sure-fire odds
of a million to one

the dog in the barber's swallows the hair and is sick

this 3 for 2 offer one's not enough   three you can't carry
two they won't let you   the thing is impossible
leave it   give up   give it up
but not forgetting

bundling in the open door
you come bearing
a pint of milk for the tea
and a bag for life

The Silk of the Seas and the Arctic Flowers

The last drop of petrol always like the last drop of pee, shaken out and going to waste. King Billy on his steed, over the gents': our great deliverer; stirrupless Caesar of the all-night disco bar and two-for-one offer on the alcopops. It was here I felt the call of the river, the need to look on its vicious majesty and be comforted once more. So I drove, I found the station playing the one pop song in the world able to save us and drove. Look at that sun in your eyes: take it and break it and leave it in fragments spilling the daylight into the earth. On the traffic island lives a white-tailed rabbit who will marry the owl and the pussycat and wave them off to sea, to a fly-past from the Airfix factory down the road and corks popped at the cod liver oil place beyond that. You want hard, I'll give you hard; want letters home about bed bugs and scurvy, that's what you'll have; want can't be bothered, meet me out here after closing time in a party hat and fake nose. This afternoon the sky has decided to take the Zeebrugge ferry and won't be returning, dragging the waders and ducks behind it. That's another half-dozen off my twitcher's list: see them once, I tell myself, then let them get the hell out, it's not like I want them hanging around, cluttering up the place, and off they go, wheeling and screaming. A half hour of this and I've sunk up to my binoculars in this quagmire, and are you trying to pull me out or offering to come down with me, you'll have to shout louder than that if this is going to make any sense. Or bundle me into the boot, release the bawdy handbrake's grip and leave me to smother in the mudbanks' glutinous kiss. So here we are then, here I stand and gaze on the river and know I am right, Midnight and Fugly the Fort Paull owls whispering one in each ear, telling me so. Take my hand and close the boot with me from inside: here in the dark, the warm, the wet, never more certain all our lives, of what I don't know, I've no idea, but something, something, certain, certain.

Nationwide

The slow fuse amber and black
of match day's three o'clock shout
files past us
along the bridge

everything in its right place
for an early season grudge tie
Northern realism
v. estrangement effect

the cinder path and the chimney
are certain starters the railway
has been deemed
ineligible

there are crab apples in the garden
behind the hospital and a domino
row of tower blocks
if required

the first side to give up the struggle
will be declared victors
the crowd will be
ferocious yet fair

its cheering follows us up the street
as we make our way home: a small
puppy dog we pick up
and carry

hours later taking the bin out
we find it running in circles
in the back garden
and think

of the crab apple harvest

perfect red inedible   going
to waste and
rightly so

Shorts

A Dying Animal

lifted

its empty waterbowl
heavier in my hand

than the full

as if

a shadow
alone casts
no shadow

departing to no
goodbye it
can receive
or return

it goes
without saying

Something Understood

I hear you
listen

The Tannery

Hideless, they pace the tannery yard,
ghosts of cattle we do for like cattle,
watching us walk in their footsteps:
bits and pieces of them marched down
our escape routes from our own skin
disguised as them, disguised as ourselves.

Thomas Hardy, Poems 1912-13

as in the beginning

waiting

to find

each other

wanting

On Not Translating

We swam a river from opposite banks,
met halfway and kept going.
There was no awkwardness.
We did not have words.

Tears

after René Char

Tears despise their confidant.

Christmas Trees

In lapsed honour of the some other time
arrival of a god not mine
bin day finds the grass verge strewn
with stripped brown trees in a tatty line
celebrating nothing and no one.

In Memoriam György Ligeti

stone plus
just enough

missing gives
ocarina plus

just enough
breath gone

missing
its song

Untitled

Hullabalooza

hell of a boozer

lovable loser

Rag and Bone

Poor old, tired old horse,
patiently dragging what must
feel like his own hearse.

Have You Seen This Cat?

Because it is awesome.

(found)

Little Soul

Little soul
  drooling boy
hot water bottle

tucked into your skin
  when you resurface
from sleep

two dark moons
  rise perfectly into
the eye-sized holes

in your fur.

From the English

An Bhadhbh

(ó Beckett)

a hocras á streachailt léi trí spéir
mo chloiginn blaosc an spéir's an chré

á umhlaidh fein do na bacaigh a bheas orthu
ualach na beatha a árdú is siúil leis

iad ina gceap magaidh ag an gcolainn
go n-iompóidh ocras cré agus spéir ina ndramhaíl

An Ghreabhróg

Mí Márta arís agus airimíd
greabhróg ag teacht i dtír
ar an gcé ar an bhfál cúng
idir a himeacht anuraidh
is filleadh na bliana seo chugainn.

An Clamhán

Codladh níor sáimhe riamh
ag an luch san aiteann amh

seachas i dtobainne ar foluain
dó ós cionn an chuain

is mar bhog-chliabhán
aige ingne an chlamháin.

Already Since Always

after André Frénaud

The dead insects' thin solemn noise
in the confiding greenery.
The current's fragile momentum.
The hawthorn's slow foam.
The pathways driven into the sky.

The throughther splashes, the journeys gone missing.
The first closed space, abandoned, with millstones.
O meagre prairie, heart cranking up.
Afresh without end in the vertical sun
the mountains sleeping askew, that warning.
And the seizure foreknown, the murmur.
That still-deferred threshold… content.
The breath that stirred. The uncertain, poured out.
The stains spreading, the haven forgotten.
The splendid asylum within your haunches.
The siege and the trap. The broken bridge.
The final approach.

It was the time when the coarse idols crumbled
before God's tender hilarity.

Prosopagnosia

after Pierre Reverdy

a little light
you see a rushlight
descend to light up your stomach
a woman is a rocket's arc
down there a shadow is a reader
her bare feet couldn't be prettier

cardiac short-circuit
flames leap from the bonnet
what magnet keeps me stuck on
this wrong turn my eyes and my love have taken

a nothing a fire we light that dies
enough of the breeze
enough of heaven
all in the end's a phantasm even
your mouth and yet
where your hand falls I race with heat
you open the door and I don't go through

I see your face and can't believe it's you
pale one the vigil we kept
that night we lay on a suitcase and wept
to the sound of men laughing
half-naked urchins stravaguing
the water was transparent
a red copper wire bled radiance
the sun and your heart are one substance

Here's Looking at You

after Henri Michaux

Those who see me coming.
Me too, I'm onto them.
One day the cold will speak.
The cold will push the door open on Nothing.
And then, my hearties? What then?
Backsides to the wind, still swaggering,
bloated with others' voices and the lungs of the age,
I see the whole pack of you under one cover.
Hard at work? The palm tree shakes its arms.

And you combatants, soldiers of good heart, sold and unpaid.
Your glorious cause is beneath you. It'll be cold
in history's corridors.
How cold it is!
I see you be-aproned, and oh what a sight!
I see Christ too, and why not?
As he was two millennia back.
His beauty fading already.
His face gnawed by the kisses of Christians to come.
So are we still on for selling those seats in heaven?
I'm off then all, goodbye, my foot's on the escalator already.
Slán!

In East Park

By day, in the pool,
where the teals splash,
the hottentot teals,

to the sound of the peacocks,
peacocks in heat,
and the curassow,

the firework bird going off
with a bang, it
happens, all of it

happens, and I
will not say what,
while the guinea pigs

scatter, their necks
and backsides
as one, decide

it's worse over there
and come back,
envying the orange

bishop his perch, and how
to him too it happens:
but why spell it out,

what with the peacocks
in heat, the curassow's
screech like a whoopee

cushion deflating,
and the llamas tossing
and trotting, happens

too freely
and indistinctly
for misunderstanding,

the one thing necessary,
whatever it was;
that guinea pig has it,

he's getting away,
and don't expect help
from a peacock in heat,

but now I remember,
it all comes back now,
and if only

the curassow's song
would leave me
in peace, or I could

just see you
(are you still there?)
through the peacock's

fanned tail, there is nothing,
nothing, I would
rather discuss.

Air Street Fugue

and it breathes and it twitches   and lives

an industrial eclogue
          rancid yet green

          odour of flowering skullcap

          the air powder-coated
                              and shot-blasted

          into textures   of marvel

          circulated   recirculated
                    sculpting themselves to my lungs

          here where green-jacketed
                    young offenders

shackled in pondweed
          clear the drain

          and a green thought
abolishes all that's mard

                    moorhens nest
          and the locked-in Alsatian

          plants the strawberry
of its snout   under the fence

          the padlocked cemetery
will not have you   alive or dead

                    and what of it

          bury yourself in the air as you go

your steps repeat themselves in your skull

you have been over this way before now

there is only so much concrete
left to cover the cracks

when even the tanner's yard's

turning up green

the algae and oxidised pipework

festering green

of which I ask you

what does it mean to love
dereliction if not
seeding
this cherished boredom with ever
more of itself
and only these few stale blooms
to show for it all

the whimper of who
but the sex fiends users and vagrants
here beyond
street lights
and CCTV
or if not
if only
escape

on a stray cygnet's
trail of chevrons
follow me

writ in water

then into the briars

and asylum gained

with barely a splash

In Search of the Tenderer Thorns

Wait for the change in the tide where the Ouse meets the Trent and the Humber is born. Sound your foghorn once and slip down the jetty, where a tethered goat flicks its ears in the breeze and skitters a volley of piss in your general direction. These parishes, their runnelled fields all alluvial warping and tillage, secrete their tidal glue round your feet, and the scabby-legged cockerels in the bend of the road have spied you, Phrygian caps a red shock of sedition. Follow them twice round the mulberry bush and into the churchyard: follow the late poet squire of Yokefleet's cigarette tip in the distance like a will o' the wisp across the 'fructuant marsh', and stumble into the arms of a barman out beating the bushes on pressgang duty for the Tuesday night darts team. Stand everyone at the Hope & Anchor a drink, and that grass, that mistcircled grass on the dyke, cock an ear for its whisper under the jukebox and the farm dog barking half a mile down the road. Have you come about the interview for church warden, someone will ask. Are you that pigfeed salesman, someone will ask. No pigs around here, or hadn't you noticed. Plenty of moles though. Match on tonight then? That island out in the estuary, what is its name, the island out where the freighters pass and the avocet dips and wades: it's a trick of perspective, you're on the island, you're in the nature reserve, you're already drifting out to sea with the estuary mud; there is no island and never was, the goat has progressed to chewing its tail, you slip back on board, sound the foghorn again and disappear into the chaos beyond the last high tide. And a couple of pound coins in the change, love, for the condom machine in the jakes, and a packet of crisps. Where the Ouse meets the Trent and the Humber is born, that swaying grass, that mistcircled grass.

Bittern Étude

Listen
I know you are there
the eyes of the hide
unclip open
you are walking
out of sight
in microtones
and diminished octaves

the wind is singing
and the tune is beyond me

the path from your nest
to the water forms
a twelve-tone sequence
only you follow
the splayed feet going
chromatically there
there and there

your splash
untuning the far thud
of rush hour to natural static
this is not music
this is what
will have been music
after   wait
and it does not come

one call away
who do not call
not yet
you
subtlest most hidden
long neck scything
what escapes you

by reedbed isthmus or lake

stationed over
                the Brigid's cross
of your nest of reeds showing
        concealing
        a clutch of deep olive
                eggs

where have I not   looked for you
        for the moment
        your camouflaged eye
                breaks cover

        listened for you
spirit of the haunted milk bottle
        sunk in the centre
                of your slow-
expanding rippling
        if only
                but unheard
booms!

        and I clip shut the eyes
of the hide
                stand in the dark
        and is this not blindness?
                        this is not
blindness I am
                the last image
        on the retina
                        of a closed eye
in darkness
                there is nothing
to hear and this
        is music

Rag and Bone Man's Mild

after Baudelaire

Past the blue of the takeaway light grilling
flies for tea, where North Sea breezes roll in,
rattling the glass, out of some blind alley
where the tide of squalor rises daily,

comes, nodding his head, obscurely wise,
a rag and bone man, punching the walls as he goes,
flicking the law the finger on his patch
and holding forth to all from his royal coach.

Shouting the odds, he puts the world to rights,
gunning for wrong 'uns but looking out for mates:
huge on the throne and slicing the sky in half,
What a top bloke I am, he tells himself.

Canny lads, dodging social services,
do his bidding, as charming as they're vicious,
and chuck the fridges, tellies, bikes, on back,
all Bankside's indiscriminate bric-a-brac,

and so wind home, merry and victorious,
hailing their way down back-street terraces.
Every last tattoo's a campaign medal
for these veterans of old scrap metal,

with yards as rich as Ali Baba's cave
awaiting them and a fry-up on the stove,
and then a night on the tear to music pounding,
the lasses game, the pub-crawls never-ending.

Lubricating this daft life of theirs,
singing his exploits through their drunken roars
but needing only froth before he's crowned,
flows king mild, a rich brown river current,

the balm of idlers, stopping their mardy gobs
till chucking out time when they phone for cabs
to dump them home to sleep – but who needs sleep
when there's mild to drink, dark and true and deep!

2885160R00017

Printed in Great Britain
by Amazon.co.uk, Ltd.,
Marston Gate.